White Orchids

Ry Reed

White Orchids

Ry Reed

Ry Reed Books ©

Thank you so much for buying this book! Thank you so much for buying this book! Don't forget to leave a review. I want you to share your thoughts with the world.

Thank you!

Books by Ry Reed

Poetry

<u>PINK GRAPEFRUIT</u>

<u>WHITE ORCHIDS</u>

<u>GREY STORM CLOUDS</u>

<u>THE LITTLE RED POETRY BOOK CALLED HEARTBREAK</u>

<u>WALKING ON THE MOON</u>

<u>A WELL OF THOUGHTS</u>

I originally wrote White Orchids for me.

I needed to motivate myself. Sometimes I contemplated quitting writing, and these poems changed my life. Then it hit me. I'm not the only person on this planet struggling. I figured sharing what I've learned with you would be a good idea.

So, to you, my reader, and new friend, if you're trying to discover a passion, working on them, and can't decide if you should follow your dreams or have already taken the plunge, keep at it! Work on your dreams every day. Surround yourself with people who love and support you. Find moments to be alone to develop your craft. And don't forget to celebrate every milestone. That's very important to do. Every small victory deserves a celebration.

Good luck and too many more wins,

Cheers.

Keep hitting the same rock until water flows from it.

-Ry Reed

CONTENTS

Books by Ry Reed   4

CONTENTS   7

Dream big   21

Dangerous men in wait   22

How long change takes…   23

Born dreamers   24

Relatives   25

Be patient even with the little things.   26

Standing on tippy toes   27

Watch the seasons go by   28

I know you can do it   29

Go buy a journal   30

It's called procrastination   31

You are a story waiting to be discovered   32

Your today starts right now   33

Lies we believe   34

Self-doubt   35

The selfish one   36

Imagination-Os   37

The painter   38

You never know   39

Time is of the essence   40

Childhood wonder   41

Marvelous creatures   42

Dreams to reality   43

Born fishermen   44

8 a.m. traffic   45

Chicken…   46

First day of…   47

Usurper   48

The bird who never met the sky   49

Ghost of the current past   50

Foot physiology   51

The truth   52

Easily swayed   53

The first step   54

Get to work   55

Weight scale   56

Youthful spirit   57

Just your imagination   58

Pandemonium   59

Rose colored lens   60

Sirius   61

The greatest pretender   62

Four corners   63

Your story begins   64

Black and white   65

Master designer   66

Sowing seeds   67

Today   68

First lap   69

Time sensitive   70

Mapquest   71

Short stories   72

Gear up   73

REM   74

Pocketwatch   75

Never settle for less   76

Why not   77

Pain tolerance   78

Mason jar   79

True mirror 80

Scared 81

Ry Reed said 82

Dawdle 83

PLANTING SEEDS 86

Architect 87

Subconscious mind 88

All in 89

Goldrush 90

Growing season 91

Sunflower seed 92

Wishing well 93

Mud 94

Cookbook 95

Life questions 96

New lineage 97

The process 98

You answer 99

Proactive 100

Patience vs. impatience 101

Monday morning 102

A letter to the haters 103

Bloody pride   104

Dream killer   105

The human condition   106

Moses' apprentice   107

Greatness   108

Coming my way   109

Time to leave the nest   110

uncomfortable   111

Hardships   112

Goodbye mother   113

Would you believe me   114

Barren harvest   115

A complete waste   116

Sore wrists   117

The five year plan   118

Journey   119

Foreign comforts   120

Let's get serious   121

Your dreams did take root. You just can't see them
yet   124

Greatest impact   125

Pregnant   126

Waiting   127

My race   128

Weather forecaster   129

I just learned this   130

Thieves and villains   131

These are the rules   132

Grammy   133

Ask him   134

It's lonely   135

My story   136

Secret sauce   137

Existence   138

Find it   139

Dreams in motion   140

Friends of faith   141

Push   142

Starting line   143

6 a.m.   144

Your fault   145

I once knew a man   146

Five years   147

Hair cuts   148

Time will   149

I'm the problem   150

Wake up early   151

Wipe tears   152

Off her porch   153

Let them go   154

Lone ranger   155

Define failing   156

Behind the scenes   157

Gratification   158

Grandma   159

Miscarriage   160

Take Root   162

Will and won't   163

Professional   164

Storms   165

Just breathe   166

Frustration   167

Crossroads   168

Define tenacity   169

Scarecrows keep fear away   174

Galaxies   175

Let them know   176

Battle ready   177

Right   178

Take it easy   179

Quitters   180

Protection system   181

You'll see   182

Right way   183

Scary movie   184

Mind your beesiness   185

Figure it out   186

Immature   187

Standstill   188

Made for war   189

The next day   190

Listen to yourself   191

Eat up   192

I said it   193

I went there   194

Contently uncontent   195

Bedhead   196

A lifetime's wait   197

Weeds in your garden 201

Pug 202

Atlantis 203

Those people 204

Vampires 205

To themselves 206

Bad company 207

Scaredy cat 208

Light bill 209

Elon 210

Judas 211

Weedkiller 212

Continue on 213

A wall 214

Write a response 215

Check for fangs 216

Support group 217

Yup 218

Happy people 219

Careless men 220

Loverboy 221

Pack life 222

Remote control 223

A very hard truth 224

Waves goodbye 225

Reading glasses 226

Scavenger 227

Mingle 228

Proud mama bear 229

Hercules 230

Warning label 231

Write what you feel 232

Be gone 233

Write a response 234

Write a response 235

Write a response 236

Write a response 237

When droughts come 241

Anchor 242

Rock climber 243

Green tea 244

Cinderella 245

1% 246

Sealife 247

Reminisce   248

Sedan   249

Prepare for war   250

Head above water   251

A strong grip   252

Power mode   253

I don't like Monday   254

Well rounded woman   255

I thought   256

You can…   257

Road bumps   258

Inner fire   259

Investigate   260

Curveball   261

Bus stop   262

Earth bender   263

Concentrate   264

Minor scars   265

Tell them   266

Glue   267

I will do   268

Knobby knees   269

Real talk	270
Think about it	271
Patiently grow your garden	275
Slow cooked	276
Have gentle hands	277
The longest winter	278
Brewery	279
Be resilient	280
My mother's recipe	281
While you wait	282
Walking dead	283
Conditioning	284
Write, please	285
Bricks and mortar	286
To do list	287
Play by play	288
In style	289
Castle by the ocean	290
Brainpower	291
Overnight	292
Alarm clock	293
Flower girl	294

Definition of patience	295
One day	296
Skywatcher	297
Seed form	298
6:30 a.m.	299
Door to door	300
Home alone	301
Galileo	302
Busy Friday	303
Task setting	304
Honeybee	305
Midas touch	306
African Proverb	307
Wisest man	308
First signs of life	312
Life advice	313
Second wind	314
Believe	315
About the author	318
Ry Reed's social media	324

Your dreams are seeds

Dreams always begin small.

But,

They don't have to remain that size,

If you dream like a giant

Dream big

If you share your vision with the wrong soul

He/she might step on it.

Dangerous men in wait

It takes 21 days to start a new habit.

How long change takes...

Don't expect everyone to see the same thing

You see in the clouds

It takes a great deal of imagination

To envision

More

Born dreamers

Sometimes, diamonds are mistaken

For glass.

Remember this

When you cash out on

Your diamonds

And they stick out their hands

Asking you for some

Relatives

She didn't know any better. A seed. Just a little seed. Why she was hungry today. Today she was hungry. Today she was poor. Today she needed shade from the burning sun. She planted all she owned. And waited…and waited…and waited. On the fourth day, when nothing came out of the ground, she abandoned her opportunity in search of already flourishing gardens in the west. Exactly three years from this day, she returned to the seed she left and saw more fruit than she had sowed. But, a gate perched high around her dream, with a wooden sign, was hung for incoming visitors not to walk on the new owner's property.

Be patient even with the little things.

It's when she stood on a rock

She could see over the manmade fence

Blocking her horizon.

Standing on tippy toes

Everything wonderful starts small. So don't rush a seed into being a tree before it's ready.

Watch the seasons go by

Never give up.

I know you can do it

Any time a good idea comes to you,

Write it down before you

Forget it.

Go buy a journal

Coming up with an idea is the easy part.

Working on it

Is the part

Most people

Don't do

It's called procrastination

You are creative

You are a genius

There are adventures

Within your veins

Waiting to unfold

You are a story waiting to be discovered

Age has nothing to do with deciding…

Deciding to follow your passions

Deciding to put yourself out there

Deciding to do what you love

Despite what your family or friends think is powerful.

This is your life

And you only get one life

To do the impossible

Baby, don't you waste this opportunity

Your today starts right now

She wasted the last four years of her life

Contemplating chasing butterflies in sharp thorns

Only if she knew that

Thorns do not kill

Thorn's scarp and tear

But they do not kill

Lies we believe

Don't talk yourself out of a good idea.

Self-doubt

Why hold onto something

You were born to share,

That's selfish

The selfish one

The world needs your particular brand of imagination.

Imagination-Os

You were created

To dream dreams

Into existence.

The painter

You never know…

You never know who is silently waiting to meet you

You never know can't move on until you talk to them

You never know who is lost and is anticipating your compass

You never know whose life will change the instant you arrive

You never know.

That's why it's so important you go after

Your dreams because you never know whose life you will change

You never know

It's not time to act small.

Time is of the essence

She's powerful, you hear me.

So strong, and her arms could wrestle gators

Her legs hiked glaciers

She once told me she stung a bee

While slugging an oak tree

To Pittsburg

On a side errand to free women

Stranded in Philly

Trapped in a blizzard.

She politely told a newscaster

It was only breezy

The cold thought she was cold

Then she walked home

She did these miraculous things in her dreams

Never, in reality, you see.

Childhood wonder

Your mind is full of beautiful thoughts.

Marvelous creatures

If you are reading this book

And are contemplating

Starting (blank)

Well, why don't you?

Doing (blank) has been on your mind

For far too long.

You've told everybody about doing (blank),

You dream of (blank) all day,

Well, why don't you?

Dreams to reality

She knew she was a sailor

And,

Her mother would dress her

In pink and white floral prints

On early Sunday mornings

To eat brunch before a lavish

Band of suited men and

Church lady hatted women.

Whenever she heard the

Ocean waves roughing the rocks

Off the coast,

She would ever so slightly swan

Her neck for just a glimpse

Before a waiter would ask her

To place an order...

Rum she said

Born fishermen

Standing in the same place for too long

Ensures achy bones

A tired back

Sagged shoulders

And bored eyes

8 a.m. traffic

I couldn't imagine being a bird that never flew....

Chicken...

The water isn't that cold

Once you jump in

Of course,

Initial shock ruins the experience

In the beginning.

You'll learn to get over it.

First day of…

Ideas come and go

They'll go if you

Don't catch them

They'll float into another

Man/woman's hands

Then, you'll never get

Your ideas back

Usurper

Standing on a ledge to possible doom

Is how doubt rots your mind

It makes you turn from ever jumping

Forward

Because doubt doesn't want you

To realize that

You have wings.

The bird who never met the sky

She lived beneath sticks longer than

She should have.

That very awareness

Haunted her.

"Why didn't I go sooner?"

Plagued her.

Ghost of the current past

Feet

Are

There

To

Explore

With.

Foot physiology

Everyone's opinion does not matter

In the long run.

Their opinion is not your identity.

It's best you hear this from me.

The truth

She asked her father what lies behind

A mountain blocking the sun

He told her nothing

She believed him,

Agreeing never to travel

Uphill again

Easily swayed

Write your dreams down

So they'll turn into goals.

The first step

Wishing on a star is nice and all

But taking the first step forward

Is how shooting stars

Become catchable

Get to work

You won't know how strong you are

Until you start lifting weights

Weight scale

Where did it go? Your untamed spirit?

That oh-so-youthful fire?

You used to be that girl

Who went up the slide

In the wrong direction

The boy dared to eat ants on the playground

Chaser of fast cars on a bike

The I'm going to jump off the roof and see what happens

Push me in a grocery cart, and I don't give a damn

If they kick us out

Ding dong ditch past my bedtime

I'm going to steal my mom's car to pick you up…

Where did that outgoing spirit go?

You used to try new things?

You were never afraid of what people thought of you

You allowed yourself to be all sides of yourself

Can she/he come out again?

Youthful spirit

Be the dreamer who dreamed dreams into reality

Just your imagination

You learn to be afraid of the dark

When someone tells you to be.

Naturally, the dark wasn't

Your initial fear.

Pandemonium

You're not as small as you think.

Rose colored lens

It seems like stars are too far from our hands

To ever be ours to own

It's when you stretch your arms and fingers

Now,

You're a little bit closer.

Sirius

A ballerina should never pretend to be a construction worker.

A construction worker shouldn't pretend to be a painter.

A painter shouldn't pretend to be a doctor.

A doctor shouldn't pretend to be a rock climber.

A rock climber shouldn't pretend to be a restaurant owner.

A restaurant owner shouldn't pretend to be a ballroom dancer.

If you're not passionate about what you're doing,

You shouldn't do it.

The greatest pretender

You will appreciate walking in grassy fields

If you've been trapped in a box all your life.

Four corners

Discover your purpose.

Your story begins

I've painted in shades of gray and white and black

The problem,

There are more colors than gray and white, and black.

Black and white

A flower loses its purpose

If no one

Takes the time

To smell

It's life's work.

Master designer

You'll never know

What sort of flower you are

Until you plant

A piece of your soul into the ground

And watch yourself grow.

Sowing seeds

Whether you are 8 or 88

There is air in your lungs

Blood flowing through your heart and limbs

You woke today

And tomorrow is not promised

But there is today.

Today.

Today.

Today.

Today

Start and

Do not quit.

First lap

There is time

When you make time

To take on

The things

You've always admired.

Time sensitive

This world is neither flat nor flows in one direction

There are multiple directions

To pick

Just in case you get lost

Maps are easy to purchase

Mapquest

Even the tiniest of us have important stories to tell.

Short stories

You only lose when you decide not to play.

Gear up

Become your wildest dream.

REM

You're not dead, so you still have time.

Pocketwatch

Why live a life you regret living?

Why not live a life full of choices

You'll never regret making?

Never settle for less

Like my father told me, "You never know, so you might tis well make some money if you think it will make you money."

Why not

Life is full of hurts.

It will hurt if you choose to stand exactly where you're at for the rest of your life

And,

It will hurt failing, falling, and getting back up.

Pick the hurt with the biggest reward.

Pain tolerance

You're so much bigger than you realize

That's why you feel frustrated

Because where you're at

There isn't enough room for your roots to spread

And living in a box is slowly killing you.

Mason jar

I've lived in a box

With no lid

For all my life.

It was when

I straightened

My back

And stood

That I saw

Somewhere

Else

I

Would

Rather

Be.

True mirror

What do you call a butterfly that doesn't fly?

Though he was born with wings?

Scared.

Scared

I know

This poetry book

Hits real hard

And you're considering

Jumping on that business idea

Everyone in your life thinks is lame.

Well,

Forget them cause Ry Reed

Believes in your lame

Business idea.

Ry Reed said

Jump off the ledge when you feel ready, but don't wait too long.

Dawdle

Write

What goals do you want to begin working on?

Write

This is your dream board. Write down five things you want to accomplish this year. Big or small. Pick goals you can achieve, and don't be afraid to stretch yourself. You can do anything with the right attitude and a drop of faith.

PLANTING SEEDS

How do you build a house?

One brick at a time

One wall at a time

One roof

One door

One window

At a time.

Architect

Cradle them close to your chest

Feel their hearts beat

Living entities

Fragments of chances

Mesmerizing escapes

To portals

Creased deep within your

Conscious

Screaming to "BE!"

Be what you've imagined yourself to be

Subconscious mind

Life is all about taking risks.

Believing in an idea and running with it.

Yeah, risks are scary,

You might lose,

But you'll never

Know what you're capable of

Until you give it a try.

All in

If an idea sticks with you

For more than three months

It's a sign

You're sitting on gold

Goldrush

Pour all that you are

Into a single aspiration.

It will grow

On its own time

Slow

Or

Fast

Depending on how patient you are.

Growing season

We are all born with seeds.

Dreams are seeds.

Sunflower seed

A wish is bubbled hope thrown to the wind, relayed to nothing because you do not act upon it.

Wishing well

The first step is to soften the ground

Dig a ditch of precise size

Place life into its center

Bury

Water

Water for months to years

Patience

Then a miracle will grow.

Most people lose enthusiasm once they

Realize they must

Get dirty to receive.

Mud

Conquering your fears and starting are the secrets to success.

Cookbook

What do you want

And,

What will you do to have it?

Life questions

She rose before the sun. She drank a piping hot cup of hope and stirred a pinch of faith to sweeten the brew to her liking. She cracked her sore back. It had been a tiring first few days, and this was the last. Gardening was not an art anyone in her family was taught to love. Her kin assumed it was too risky and looked messy. She is the first gardener in her family and the first to witness a harvest.

New lineage

Think about this,

For a seed to become a tree

It must be buried in the dirt.

A seed has to live in a cold

Uncomfortable environment,

Sometimes, for years

Endure the weight of pushing upwards

Even though it has no idea where it's going

But a seed knows never to give up...

The process

Why do we quit the minute life gets hard?

You answer

Burying your purpose in the ground doesn't ensure anything.

Watering your purpose

Will bring

You more wealth

Then you'll know

What to do with it.

Proactive

Patience will be your greatest friend, and impatience will destroy the best of you if you let impatience win.

Patience vs. impatience

Life is hard. Waking up early is hard. Working on your days off is hard. Staying up late is hard. Creating content no one sees is hard. Being consistent is hard. Having a good attitude is hard. Resisting surrendering is harder. And it's only Monday.

Monday morning

Raise your hands

Ball them into fists

When they swing

Be prepared to hit back

You're not going anywhere.

Let them know that.

A letter to the haters

Bleed, but don't let them know it hurts.

Bloody pride

Did you come this far to give up?

That's not fair

Your ambitions didn't give up on you

Your dreams didn't find better people

To console

Your dreams stayed with you, and they'll die with you

Until you take the plunge.

You owe your dreams that

Dream killer

It's always when you want something more problems find you. The thing is, problems will always find you because problems enjoy ruining good days. Since problems are a part of the human condition, this should inspire you to continue and not play the victim.

The human condition

Keep hitting the same rock until water flows from it.

Moses' apprentice

Questioning whether or not you should be doing [insert] is okay

Don't you think greats questioned their actions

Before they became great

We call them greats for following through

Don't we?

Greatness

Good opportunities are

Coming my way.

Money is coming my way.

Chances to invest are coming my way.

New ideas are coming my way.

Coming my way

You might be the only one in your family ready to fly. That's okay. Be a good example.

Time to leave the nest

To grow, you must be uncomfortable. When you're too comfortable, learning doesn't take place.

uncomfortable

Every hardship is like a weight. The more difficulties you endure, the stronger you will be.

Hardships

She hugged her mother. A good hug that stole her mother's breath. Her mother wasn't into goodbyes. Women on her mother's side thought goodbyes meant "I won't see you soon." She cherished that belief and passed it on to her kin. She was ready, bags packed with things she might need: a telescope to gaze upon the stars on lonely nights, a lighter to warm her when the cold visited, and the cold would visit, a canteen for storage and such. She packed light and left her mother's worries on the doorstep. She craved to "figure it out." In the dark, in the dreary rain, she would figure it out and not return until her arms were gleaming with orange gold bracelets and pounds of powdered silver to hold "them" over for another year. She had to. They were hungry.

Goodbye mother

What if I said you're a millionaire?

Would you believe me?

What if I told you it takes one idea to generate

A million dollars?

Would you believe me?

What if I said you have a lot of ideas

That can make you a million dollars?

Would you believe me?

Would you believe me

Most plant seeds in the ground

And dig them up

Before they become anything

Because we're frustrated

Then complain about starving…

Barren harvest

It's like starving but refusing to do something about it...

It's like being born with a map you won't read...

A gifted builder choosing to rent for the rest of his life...

To own a grocery store but expect people to give you nourishment...

When you don't use your gifts, it's a complete waste.

A complete waste

Sore wrists

And calloused skin

It tells me a lot about your

Character.

You're a doer,

Not a dreamer.

Sore wrists

Suffer now, reap later.

The five year plan

This won't be an easy journey. You will get a few bruises along the way.

Journey

You grow when you're uncomfortable because you're fighting for foreign comforts no one in your family has ever seen. You'll be the first in your family to show them how. You'll be able to motivate them when they take their first step into hell and their last step to freedom.

Foreign comforts

How you spend your time reflects your success

: How you manage your time determines where you will be and where your focus lies. If you feel like you should be more ahead, track your every hour and change your schedule. You'll be amazed by how much time you waste doing activities unrelated to your dreams.

Let's get serious

Write

Is fear holding you back from going after your goals?

Write

Write down all your fears. Once you're done, face them.

Your dreams did take root. You just can't see them yet

What's not seen always has the greatest impact.

Greatest impact

A mother knows life grows within her womb

Because she can feel subtle changes

Evolving and manifesting physically and spiritually

Too soon to hold what she's creating,

She knows, one day, she will give birth to something

Miraculous,

Even if the world doesn't understand

Her incubating ambitions.

Pregnant

You've done the hard work,

Planted

Now it's time to do the painstaking work

Waiting.

Waiting

I am running my race.

I will not compare myself to others

Because I'm still developing.

It might take me longer to get there,

But I'm prepared to give it my all.

My race

Stay outside during a storm long enough

You'll be able to see when it leaves.

Weather forecaster

You have to work on

Your dreams every day

If you want them to come true.

I just learned this

Protect what little you've gathered

From dangerous thieves

And conniving villains

Hell bent on luring you

Away from guaranteed wins.

Thieves and villains are notorious

Judges.

Thieves and villains

.

Your goals must be clear and concise and come with a deadline.

These are the rules

Before it was a song, it was a melody he sang alone in his free time.

Grammy

Ask a bud if he'll allow the wind

To rob him of his destiny.

He'll tilt away from you

And continue strengthening his grasp.

Ask him

It's a lonely ride when soul and sanity pour into a hole, buried from your eyes, and told to stand by until something extraordinary emerges. They never tell you how long it'll take or that family and friends will lose faith in your conquest. You'll overhear them. But it will happen months, years from now, on a bleak Monday night. You'll know it's time and see the first signs of life. It won't be much, a tiny morsel, never enough to sustain your unstable endeavors, but it will spark enthusiasm and a childish thrill to fuel expected losses in winter. Be prepared to do it all again for maybe less or maybe more.

It's lonely

A little about me: The first book I wrote was a complete flop. I laugh while writing this. My first story was decent, but I needed practice and more years of experience. I was a seed planted, watered daily, guarded against potential threats, and unbearably a seed. I contemplated giving up and pursuing other ventures until Monday night, 7:47 p.m., happened. My mother came home from work with exciting news. A little boy, my mother's friend's son, purchased and read my book every night before he went to bed. My first buy! It was as if a piece of me had made contact. I remained calm, joyously exploding inside because a small boy was my first fan.

My story

Self-confidence

Is the secret

Sauce.

Secret sauce

Just because you can't see it

It doesn't mean it doesn't exist.

Existence

You have everything you need to be successful.

You just have to find it and pull it

Out of you.

Find it

Your dreams didn't die. If you're working on your grind, they didn't die.

Dreams in motion

Faith will be your best friend.

Friends of faith

Planting is a lonely process

You go in alone

Away from all you know

To a dark place

You instantly regret being

You might even try

Escaping.

It's too late

You're in here

There is no light

Now, push

That's all you got to do

Keep going

Push

Push

"Greats" had to start somewhere

They started

Where you stand right now.

Starting line

Hold on,

There will be turbulence.

6 a.m.

To start and never finish

Will crack your fragile faith

You'll end up blaming the system

Your mother/ father for never believing in you

Time to steal what little time you have

The weather

Finances…

It's your fault you never reached your potential.

Your fault

I once knew a man who dreamed of cooling fires in dry hills

Rescuing maidens in need

Fearless, he would be named mighty for swimming upstream

To save a town on the verge of agony.

Last I heard, he still dreams.

I once knew a man

Yes, it might take you five years to achieve (blank)

But would you rather waste your entire life

Not doing (blank)

Especially if doing (blank) will improve your life

And a state of mind?

Five years

I once knew a man who used to cut hair in his kitchen

He did so for many years

Diligently,

Saving

Resources,

Providing

Excellent service,

He

Was

Humble,

And

Patient.

He

Had

Hope.

He no longer cuts hair in his kitchen

Hair cuts

Let time be a good friend to you…

Time will teach you how to commit to outrageous thoughts

Time will teach you to utilize the sun and keep the moon company

Time will teach you not to fret because there are more days ahead of you

Time will teach you to schedule your days so you don't waste days

Time will teach you to celebrate victories and cry for loses

Time will teach you how important your time is

Time will

When I didn't see all my hard work flourishing

I blamed the soil I planted my ideas into

There was nothing wrong with the soil

There was nothing wrong with the water I used

To feed my plans

The problem was me

I did not like the process

I did not like the labor

I did not like the pessimistic audience in my court

I did not like rejection

I'm the problem

Wake up early. There's valuable sunlight to borrow in the morning.

Wake up early

Tears are part of the process.

Wipe tears

There was a girl, and she imagined a life far beyond paint and walls and beams and yard and homes and streets and town and city and county and state and country to be…in worlds unlike her own. She had shoes, rugged and made with genuine leather. She bought them second-hand. They used to belong to women she admired long before she knew their names or where she wanted to go. She tied such masterful lace knots. I swear, they were tighter than a captain's make. She prepared at night, packing necessities she said she needed but didn't need anything. She came to her door. It was a cold day, and no one she knew followed her lead. She prepared to go alone since these ideas have always driven her to be alone. She breathed, in through her nose, out through her mouth. This was it. As she walked on her porch to the sidewalk, a corner, a block, she regretted leaving her warm house made of paint, walls, beams, and a yard.

Off her porch

If people leave you when you're at your lowest, let them go.

They were fickled relationships

You don't need them right now

Let them go

Quite honestly, you can't bring everyone with you

This is not their journey

They did not hear your call

They won't respect your drive

How can they?

They're not risking what your giving up

You have more to lose

Lone ranger

Failing is not rejection. Failing is when you completely lose momentum and stop.

Define failing

The most important

Work

Always goes unseen

And people see what they want to see.

Behind the scenes

Instant gratification will be the death of you

If you allow it to be the reason

Why you get out of bed each morning.

Gratification

Old people aren't lying. Slow and easy does win the race.

Grandma

Your idea is in the conception phase.

Alive,

It has a heartbeat,

Knows your name,

Taking shape,

Growing fast,

Enlarging each day.

Don't rush your idea to come

Before it's ready,

Or

Risk a miscarriage.

Miscarriage

Write

Let's pick a goal you want to accomplish this year and write it down. Now, let's be strategic. When do you want to complete this goal, and what steps are needed for the dream to come to fruition? Do you need to wake up earlier? Get a new job, save money, hangouts? Be honest and authentic with yourself.

Take Root

Either you "will" or you "won't" do something. It's that simple.

Will and won't

How to get better at something:

-stick with it. Keep working on it until you've mastered that skill.

Professional

Dig your nails deep in. Storms will come to take all you've become.

Storms

Just breathe. I know it's hard. I know, my love. But stay grounded. Don't you move back a single step.

Just breathe

When you're tired, remember where you came from.

You hated being there

You were frustrated

Had no idea where you were going

Lost,

But

You swore you'd move ahead

And never bend your neck

To liken

Uncomfortable comforts.

Being too comfortable stunted you

Frustration

What are you willing to sacrifice to have what you want?

Crossroads

The definition of tenacity by Ry Reed: To flip your dirty sneakers off and run outside, despite your dad telling you he will beat your ass for going out. You're grounded like hell, but damn if you're about to take a lick'n before you enjoy being rebellious. Long live the crazy outsiders!

Define tenacity

Write

What's one thing in your life you want to change?
Where you live, how much money you make, the car
you drive, your education, who you're with? Then,
why do you want to change these things?

Write

What would make your life a little bit easier and relieve stress?

Write

Are there any areas of your life you've grown complacent in?

Write

What frustrates you?

Scarecrows keep fear away

Don't let darkness scare you

The most beautiful things

Shine in lightless universes

Galaxies

Your opinion of me is none of my business.

Let them know

Stare at it,

Grit your teeth

Fold your brow

Hold your ground and roar

Until they know you won't

Back down

Battle ready

You didn't come all this way to give up now, right?

Right

When you feel like life is getting out of control:

(just breathe)

Take it easy

There are three things I know about quitters:

1. Quitters quit because they chose not to fight.
2. Quitters will blame everyone under the sun if the journey is too tiresome, which a journey will always be.
3. Quitters enjoy failing, so they have a reason to return to stubborn habits.

Quitters

Fear is a homebody protection system

To guard in case of unavoidable threats

We fabricate in our minds

That hinders what we should be

To be who we shouldn't be.

There are too many

Doing what they shouldn't

Be doing.

Protection system

If you stand a bit taller than your doubt,

You'll see everything

Doubt was hiding from you

You'll see

You can't assume you know what's right.

No one knows what's right

Until right is proven wrong

Right way

Nothing is living underneath your bed,

That you didn't imagine there…

Scary movie

Ask a bee if he considered not flying because of what people said about him. I have a feeling he doesn't care.

Mind your beesiness

What to do when a strongly made wall

Is placed in front of you?:

Figure out how to jump over it. Even if it takes years.
You have time.

Figure it out

Don't entertain

Petty arguments with

Immature people.

Immature

When we take the proper footsteps forward,

Bad habits tend to

Yank feet back into position.

Most stay standing in place their entire life,

Like I did...

Standstill

You were made for war

Back firm and straight

Hands to wield

Feet to hurry

Eyes to see

A clever mind to strategize

And yet you think

Shuffling on the sidelines

Is called being active,

Actively watching comrades

War when you were designed to fight.

He reaps all your glory,

So you watch

Made for war

Cry, but come back to win the next day.

The next day

How you perceive yourself is far more important than how your dusty friends, timid parents, a jealous ex, defeated teacher, and cryptic social media followers perceive you. They aren't you. You're you. Your voice must be louder than there's. Your courage must be more steadfast. You will withstand. Listen to your intuition. That tiny voice within you. You have a gift, ideas, and all you need to fulfill them. I know it's hard. I know you're tired. I know, at times, you wonder why you're doing this, but what you're doing houses endless streams of possibilities only you have keys to unlock. Tune those haters out. Listen to yourself.

Listen to yourself

A lesson: What you fear will eat you because you've made yourself small enough to be devoured...

Eat up

Sometimes,

The only person holding you back

From being bigger than life

Is yourself...

I said it

The person you're running from is yourself…

I went there

I met a man

He loved to sing

He would sing to everything

Whether small or large

Children in the parks

Women jogging with pets

He sang to the dimming sun

Serenading loved one's goodbye

To the sick, he sang his very best

When he was down on his luck

His songs were the most heartfelt

I asked him if he would ever sing

On a stage to millions

So he could sing to everyone all day

He declined

Because he contently uncontenly

Rather sing for no one for the rest of his days

Contently uncontent

Dreamers never stop dreaming

When they realize

It's easier to dream

Then it is to

Wake up

Bedhead

How many more years are you going to spend

Staring at endless possibilities?

A lifetime's wait

Write

Who do you dream of becoming?

Write

What's holding you back?

Write

Who's holding you back?

Weeds in your garden

Fight for everything you want

Because no one wants to give

It to you.

Pug

A single lie can destroy a rising city…

Atlantis

It's those people

People who stop walking

And drag their feet in the mud

Because they feel life

Has dealt too harshly with them

They wrap their arms around

The first body they can find

And tangle their limbs

Around your limbs

Until you either trip

Or

Can no longer bear their weight

Those are the kind of people

To avoid.

Those people

If you let them, they'll suck everything good, kind, and optimistic about you.

Vampires

Just because she's your mother

Doesn't mean her hindsight is better than yours

Just because he's your father

Doesn't mean he knows more than you

Just because he's your best friend

Doesn't mean his fears are yours

They can keep their opinions to themselves

To themselves

Bad company eventually transforms into bad habits.

Bad company

Don't let people scare you out of following your dreams.

Scaredy cat

Who cares what people think of you.

Their criticism never paid your bills.

Light bill

Live to prove your doubters wrong.

Elon

Even Jesus had a few close friends he trusted,
And so should you.

Judas

Know,

Once you spot

What shouldn't be

In your garden,

Flourishing amongst

Thriving dreams,

Endless wealth,

Securities,

Vast pleasures,

I recommend plucking it out by the root.

Weedkiller

Advice: If you share something near and dear to your heart with someone you love and adore, and they dare to build false hopes and headful warnings because of their lack of accomplishments and insecurities, kindly nod, and continue with your day.

Continue on

You are allowed to construct an invisible border around yourself,

If it means preserving your optimism.

A wall

Do you feel like you're going in the right direction?

Write a response

Be careful,

Snakes like to think

They give good advice,

While secretly praying, you fail

Because they're jealous creatures.

Check for fangs

Don't always expect your friends

And family to believe in your dreams.

Sometimes, your family will be your

Harshest critics.

Know that you're onto something good,

And the right people will support you.

Support group

Worry about your business.

Yup

Unhappy people will settle and accept

Their current reality.

Happy people imagine

What can their reality be

And will do something to

Change their current

Disposition despite

Enormous obstacles.

Happy people

Once you understand how important your time is,

The less you'll waste it on people who

Could care less about your growth.

Careless men

They won't confess their intentions,

In the beginning,

They'll hide behind false teeth,

Luxury brands and imported silks,

Slick hair combs,

Ruby reds that stain lips maroon,

The image of fond kindness and servitude.

It's when you trip

He offers his hand and room to

Rest your weary head,

Locks the doors and shuts the shutters

To constrict every bit of brimming light

Out of your youthful body.

Abuse awakens something evil from within,

Then you're hunting for prey

To ruin

Like him.

Loverboy

Only hang out with lions.

They aren't afraid of anything.

Pack life

Don't let your fears control you.

Remote control

A harsh truth:

In the beginning,

Very few will care about what you're doing.

In the end,

Because there must always be an end,

They will come to count your gold.

The decision to recall their transgressions,

It's up to you, my love.

A very hard truth

To anyone who doesn't love

And respect you…

Peacefully let them go.

Waves goodbye

A woman remembers every

The hateful thing said about her

And by who.

She chooses when to

Address her haters.

Reading glasses

Scavenger

You've got too much to risk hanging out with

Negative souls.

Their poor attitudes will jack up your flow

And you'll waste too much energy dealing with

Their problem of the day

They enjoy complaining about.

Mingle

Be your biggest fan, even if nobody shows up to congratulate you on your tiniest successes. I might not know you, but I'm incredibly proud of all that you've accomplished.

Proud mama bear

This is the hardest lesson I've learned:

People will walk over you if you give them permission.

The minute you say no,

You take your power back.

Hercules

Complaining should come with a warning label.

Highly plausible

Will catch

Hindered thinking

In proximity of

Complaining spirit.

Is curable

When separated from the source

And exposed to abundant

Dosages of positivity.

Warning label

Who's holding you back?

Write what you feel

To the cynical

Emotional drainers

Darkening your sky…

They got to go!

Be gone

Are bad relationships holding you back?

Write a response

Is unforgiveness holding you back?

Write a response

Is your family holding you back?

Write a response

Are you holding yourself back?

Write a response

Write

Who hurt you? Name them…

Write

Does anyone in your life believe in your dreams? Put your name down if you can't think of anyone who believes in you.

Write

Name every positive person in your life and why they add value to you.

When
droughts
come

Floods will try to rip all you've built from you.

Cast an anchor,

Withstand the waves.

Anchor

You've hit a wall,

Now it's time

To learn how to climb it.

Rock climber

It's okay to slow down when you're tired.

Rest,

And come back when you're

Motivated and refreshed again.

Green tea

Words you should not accept:

Impossible.

Cinderella

It's only hard because you want something not everybody has.

1%

Focus on the results, not how tiresome the voyage is, because exploration will never be easy.

Sealife

You'll remember even if no one notices how far you've come.

Reminisce

I have a friend, and one day she tells me she desperately needs a car. She returned home from college, and a car would make her life easier. So, she woke up early and worked two jobs, one in the morning and one at night. She hustled. She cried. Sometimes she thought about giving up, but she wouldn't let herself quit. And every time she neared her goal amount, tragedy struck, and people came for her like never before. Unresolved debts, new bills, college payments, health issues, you name it. But she never allowed herself to quit. Today, she drives a used sedan. Not a car that stands out on the freeway, but it works for her because she remembers what she went through to buy it and what life was without it.

Sedan

It's not how she fell that matters,

It's how she rose that

Frightened them.

Prepare for war

When life gets more challenging, and you feel like drowning, either…

Float…

Or…

Drown…

Head above water

Fight to be happy

Because happiness won't

Willingly come to you.

A strong grip

Don't lose momentum.

Power mode

When you're tired,

You're not allowed to give up.

I don't like Monday

Don't be the woman

Everyone loves,

Because that's a lot of upkeep.

Be the woman you love,

Because you have to

Live with yourself.

Well rounded woman

My biggest regret was ever thinking I couldn't. I thought I was too young. I thought I was too soft. I thought I was too inexperienced. I thought I was too damaged. I thought I was too nervous. I thought I was too shy. I thought I was too small. I thought I was too insignificant. I thought I was too unapproachable. I thought I was too scared… Take all your worries and throw them off a ledge.

I thought

Giving up is not an option.

You can...

Bad times will come. They're inevitable to avoid. Trust me. I've tried. The best thing to do when life gives you too much to carry is to carry new weights with a different mindset. Say…today might be bad, but at least I have shoes on my feet and a head full of bright ideas. My car might not be in the best shape, but I still have a job. School is whipping my behind, but at least I like that one girl in class. I'm hut, but I'm moving in the right direction and will use this road bump as a step to propel me to greater heights!

Road bumps

As the temperature drops, huddle closer to yourself for inspiration.

Inner fire

To every problem, there is a solution

Waiting to be found.

Investigate

Whatever life throws at you

You can handle it.

You've got this!

You are not defeated

And you're going to come out stronger

Because you're strong.

Curveball

There's today's failure

And tomorrow's opportunities

Waiting for your arrival.

Bus stop

You can move mountains,

But today,

Practice moving hills.

Earth bender

Focus in chaos.

Concentrate

I may have failed,

But I have not lost the battle.

I got hit,

I learned an important lesson.

Now I'm ready to try again.

Minor scars

Complaining never got the job done…

Tell them

You find out how strong

You are when you're broken.

Glue

I will do whatever it takes

To go after what I want.

I'm prepared to wake up earlier,

Go to bed later,

Invest my free time,

Work on Saturdays,

Be selfish.

I will do

You learn when you fail.

So don't be too hard on yourself

When things go bad.

You're growing.

Knobby knees

Tell yourself to get out of bed,

Even if you're tired as hell

Because there's money to be made...

Real talk

You lose when you quit.

Think about it

Write

What are your greatest strengths? (Brave, kind, encouraging)

Write

What life mistakes have you learned from?

Write

What will you do to have what you want in life?

Patiently grow your garden

The best things in life never happen overnight.

It's a trapeze of insanity

A blend of tenacity

That brings forth

The best of you forward.

Slow cooked

Patiently wait for your blessing.

Have gentle hands

Don't mistake this season

For regression.

What you've planted

Is in progress

And how fast this season lasts

Depends on your willingness

To be patient.

The longest winter

Making magic is slow and tedious work

Brewery

Resilience is another form of patience.

Be resilient

We love to eat cake,

But no one likes

To slave in a hot kitchen

For hours

Buy and prep ingredients

Stir and beat mixes

Butter pans

Sit and wait by an oven

Cool for 15 minutes

Apply icing

Then serve.

My mother's recipe

You'll love and hate yourself for waiting

You'll scream and be thankful while you wait

You'll blame God and pray while you wait

You'll consider leaving and recommit while you wait

You'll cry and encourage yourself while you wait

You'll complain and seek solitude while you wait

You'll be impatient and learn from your mistakes
while you wait

You'll lose sleep and wake up early as you wait

You'll celebrate waiting once it's all over.

While you wait

Find peace of mind as you walk through the valley of death.

Walking dead

If you're wondering why life has been so hard lately, it's because you've asked life for more, and life is ensuring you're strong enough to receive what you've requested.

Conditioning

What do you want to accomplish this week? Write down a small goal, please.

Write, please

What is a wall?

Thousands and thousands

Of individual bricks

Stacked together to

Be made taller

Then its original purpose.

What does that mean?

Every time you lay down a brick

Today, tomorrow, or next year

It's slowly becoming something

More prominent in the process.

Bricks and mortar

Your priorities are important and
It's okay to put your needs first.

To do list

Outwork and outhustle

Your competition.

Play by play

Everything you do has to excite you. Initially, no one will understand your vision, but your creativity, drive, and gifts will draw crowds one day. Give the world time to catch on.

In style

Let your imagination be your fuel while waiting for your castle to be built.

Castle by the ocean

Your most powerful skill is your ability to FOCUS.

Brainpower

When you focus, you can achieve anything.

Your life will change overnight.

Overnight

You work hard because you want to live like no one else,

That's why you wake up before your alarm clock.

Alarm clock

She is a sunflower too wild for gardens.

One root in

One root out

She chases the sun

And stress free days.

Flower girl

Patience

Noun

: The capacity to accept or tolerate delay, trouble

Suffering without getting upset.

: the ability to remain calm, even if you've been waiting forever.

Syn: perseverance, tenacity, diligence, resolution, with purpose.

Definition of patience

A seed has enough confidence to know

One day,

Soon,

It will be taller than buildings.

Know one day,

You'll be just as great.

One day

Be brave enough to reach for the stars

In wondrous

Spaces

Most aren't courageous enough

To go

After.

Skywatcher

I am in seed form.

Today, I might be small,

My roots are fragile,

The slightest wind can bend me over,

But, I was born to be a mighty oak tree.

I'm taking all the time I need to sprout.

Seed form

Wake up with a plan.

6:30 a.m.

Knock on every door until someone says yes!

Door to door

You find out

Who you are

When no

One is

Around

To applaud

Your every

Stride.

Home alone

It's when you're alone

You're able

To construct

Galaxies

With just a

Thought.

Galileo

If it's Friday night

And you chose

To stay home

To work on your goals,

I'm proud of you.

Busy Friday

You win when you decide

To accomplish tasks

That will improve your life.

Task setting

What if bees were lazy

And gave up looking for pollen

Anytime they were discouraged?

Then,

You wouldn't have any honey.

Honeybee

Everything you touch will turn to gold.

Midas touch

Keys to success:

Keep learning.

Keep improving.

Keep trying.

African Proverb

Ask for more blessings than you know what to do with.

Wisest man

Write

Do you struggle with being patient?

Write

What do you want to focus on this year?

Write

What areas in your life do you want to see improvement in?

First signs of life

Be you.

People will eventually

Catch on.

Life advice

When everyone slows down and walks…

You: RUN LIKE HELL!

Second wind

She is the bravest

Woman I know

When the world

Told her no,

She proved them

Wrong

And taught

Herself how

To fly

Believe

Write

Who or what must you let go of to be the person
you've always wanted to be?

You made it to the end! Now it's time to leave a review! Share your thoughts with the world.

Thank you!

About the author

Ry Reed has written poetry for many years. Poetry has helped her heal, and she uses her life as a platform to teach and share lessons she's learned along her journey. Depression, heartbreak, and willingness to move forward and start over again, her poems are relatable, personal, and straight to the point. Her every word digs out emotions and encourages change. She lives in southern California with her mother and brothers and writes poetry, non-fiction, and fiction books.

WHITE ORCHIDS

https://ryreedthewriter.com/

ISBN: 9781676490364

ISBN: 9781078757126

ISBN: 978-0-9981459-1-4

Subjects: Poetry/Motivation/Self-Help

Summary: Ry Reed's WHITE ORCHIDS is for dreamers. Those who have lived with dreams and aspirations are ready to put their thoughts into reality. A dream (seed) always begins small, but in time, a dream (seed) will not stay a dream (seed). It can become greater than expected if you're patient enough to work on your daily goals. Use this book to jot down your dreams and focus on your priorities.

Latest Release

Ry Reed

A WELL OF THOUGHTS

The Little
Red
Poetry
Book
Called
Heartbreak

Ry Reed

Grey Storm
Clouds

Ry Reed

Pink Grapefruit

Ry Reed

White Orchids

Ry Reed

322

Walking
on
the
Moon

Ry Reed

Ry Reed's social media

INSTAGRAM: @ry.reed.the.writer

PINTEREST: Ry Reed the writer

YOUTUBE: Ry Reed the Writer

FACEBOOK: ryreedauthorandpoet

WEBSITE: https://ryreedthewriter.com/

Ry Reed Books ©

Made in the USA
Las Vegas, NV
30 June 2023

74076267R00179